GREAT ENGINEERING

BUILDING
ROADS

REBECCA STEFOFF

Cavendish Square

New York

Published in 2016 by Cavendish Square Publishing, LLC
243 5th Avenue, Suite 136, New York, NY 10016

Website: cavendishsq.com

This publication represents the opinions and views of the author based on his or her personal experience, knowledge, and research. The information in this book serves as a general guide only. The author and publisher have used their best efforts in preparing this book and disclaim liability rising directly or indirectly from the use and application of this book.

CPSIA Compliance Information: Batch #WS15CSQ

All websites were available and accurate when this book was sent to press.

Library of Congress Cataloging-in-Publication Data

Stefoff, Rebecca, 1951- author.
Building roads / Rebecca Stefoff.
pages cm. — (Great engineering)
Includes bibliographical references and index.
ISBN 978-1-50260-604-4 (hardcover) ISBN 978-1-50260-603-7 (paperback) ISBN 978-1-50260-605-1 (ebook)
1. Roads—Design and construction—Juvenile literature. 2. Civil engineering—Juvenile literature. I. Title.

TE149.S744 2016
625.7—dc23

2015002703

Editorial Director: David McNamara
Editor: Andrew Coddington
Copy Editor: Rebecca Rohan
Art Director: Jeffrey Talbot
Designer: Amy Greenan
Senior Production Manager: Jennifer Ryder-Talbot
Production Editor: Renni Johnson
Photo Research: J8 Media

The photographs in this book are used by permission and through the courtesy of: KKwan Kwanchai/Shutterstock.com, cover; Tim Roberts Photography/Shutterstock.com, 5; Joanna Zaleska/Shutterstock.com, 7; Bart Coenders/E+/Getty Images, 11; 06photo/Shutterstock.com, 12; Vadim Ratnikov/Shutterstock.com, 13; Steven Frame/Shutterstock.com, 15; Thirteen/Shutterstock.com, 17; Pi-Lens/Shutterstock.com, 18; 06photo/Shutterstock.com, 19; Vadim Ratnikov/Shutterstock.com, 20; Damon Bay/Moment Open/Getty Images, 23; 52691989/Shutterstock.com, 24; trekandshoot/Shutterstock.com, 27.

Printed in the United States of America

TABLE OF CONTENTS

CHAPTER ONE

Getting Around

Roads tie the world together. City streets are roads. So are country lanes. Huge highways packed with high-speed cars are roads, too.

People, bikes, cars, and trucks go from place to place using roads. It wasn't always that way. A long time ago, people moved around without roads.

Early humans traveled on foot. At times they followed the trails that animals made. Over time, hooves and feet wore away the grass or bushes on these trails. A narrow dirt path remained.

Highways cross over and under each other at a stacked interchange.

How did people go from using dirt paths to building modern superhighways? Road building took time. Over thousands of years, people have developed skills and learned to build the far-reaching highways we see today.

What Is a Road?

A road is any path of travel that has been improved, or made better. Even a dirt path can become a simple road if people improve it.

Imagine a path that has to twist and turn around a tree. You cut down the tree. Then you move some big rocks out of the middle of the path. You have improved the path. You have started turning it into a road.

A road makes it easier for **traffic** to move over land. Traffic is everything that travels on roads. Today, most traffic is made up of cars and trucks. Traffic on the world's first roads was very different.

The First Roads

The first roads were paths that people improved by making them wider and smoother. If a stream crossed a path, people put a log across the stream to use as a bridge.

Travelers went along these simple roads on foot. They carried goods from place to place to sell or trade. Some travelers used animals such as horses or oxen to carry loads.

Two things made people build bigger and better roads.

When people started using wheels, they needed better roads. Horses pulled chariots like this one.

One of those things was the wheel. About five thousand years ago, people in the Middle East started using carts and wagons with wheels. Over time, use of the wheel spread through Asia and Europe.

Now that people could use wagons to carry bigger loads, they needed new roads. The roads had to be wide enough for wagons. Roads also had to be covered with sand, **gravel**, or flat stones. This kept the roads from turning into mud when it rained. Wagons could get stuck in mud.

The other reason for better roads was bigger armies. Kings wanted to move their armies around.

This meant a lot of soldiers marching along at the same time. Armies could move faster on a wide, flat, smooth road than on a small track. Kingdoms with big armies started building new roads.

Roman Roads

The top road-builders of the ancient world were the Romans. They built a web of roads that tied the city of Rome, in Italy, to most of Europe. Some roads had stone bridges over rivers. Some had tunnels through steep hills.

Roman soldiers did not just use the roads. They built some of them, too. Romans made three kinds of roads. One kind was dirt that had been **graded**, or made level and smooth. One kind was graded dirt with layers of gravel on top. The strongest roads were **paved**, or covered, with blocks of stone.

Roman roads were the best in the world for hundreds of years. Some Roman roads are still in use.

Modern Roads

Today there are three main reasons to build a road. One is that roads can wear out. A new road might be built to take the place of an old one. Another reason is to put a road where no road has ever gone. That might mean building a road through a jungle, or over a mountain range.

The reason most roads are built today is because there is more traffic. More people, cars, and trucks need to use roads. That means that new or bigger roads must be built. Making a road today is a big job that takes a team of people.

CHAPTER TWO

First Steps

Before a road can be built, it must be planned. This can take longer than building the road. For an interstate highway that goes through more than one state, planning can take years.

Engineers on the Job

Engineers are the backbone of road building. An engineer is someone who turns ideas into things people can use.

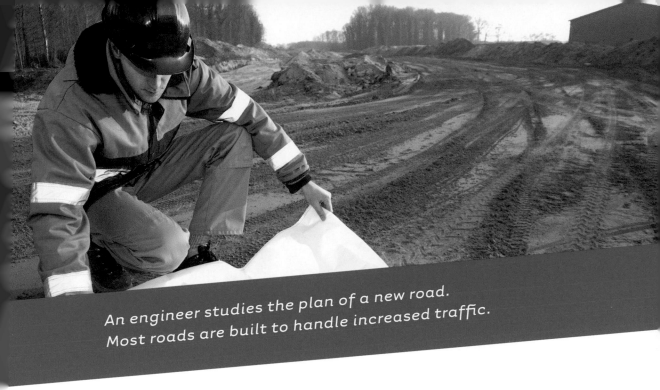

An engineer studies the plan of a new road. Most roads are built to handle increased traffic.

All engineers know some science and math. There are many kinds of engineers, such as electrical engineers and computer software engineers. Engineers who build bridges, dams, and roads are called **civil engineers**.

Civil engineers have to know about materials. Many roads are paved with **asphalt**, a sticky black form of oil. Engineers know how asphalt acts in

cold and hot temperatures. **Concrete** is another paving material. Engineers know how long it takes concrete to set, or dry.

When planning a road, engineers may want help from a **geologist**, a scientist who studies the earth and what it is made of. Geologists know about different kinds of soil and rock. They can tell whether landslides or earthquakes might happen along the new road.

Another important member of the road-building team is the **surveyor**. This expert uses special tools to measure the land. Surveyors can pinpoint the location of any spot on earth.

A surveyor checks to make sure that the new road lines up perfectly with the plan.

When roads are planned, surveyors lay out the route. They make sure that the road gets built right where it is supposed to be built.

Planning a Road

Roads can be built by cities or states. If it's a big project, the US government may be in charge. Getting ready to build a highway takes many steps.

The first step in planning is to find out how the new highway will change the land around it. Do any endangered species live where the highway will run? Will the highway destroy forests or wetlands?

The environmental review also looks at how the highway might change people's lives. Will it make a lot of traffic noise in people's houses? Will it block the way to schools or hospitals?

Scientists, lawyers, and people who live near the planned road give their thoughts. If enough of them agree, the project goes ahead.

Next, the highway is designed, or planned in every detail. How many lanes in each direction? Where will it need bridges to go over rivers? Will it need tunnels through hills? Where will the lights and safety railings be put?

PROTECTED BIRD SITE

AREA CLOSED
NO PEOPLE, DOGS,
OR VEHICLES
ALLOWED

**These Birds are Protected by
Federal and State Laws**

DO NOT DISTURB

Entry Prohibited without the Express Permission
of the Installation Commander

Road builders must avoid important parts of the environment. This area is protected for birds.

Engineers study the flow of cars and trucks in the area. They think about how much traffic might grow in the years ahead. They want the highway to be wide and thick enough to handle the traffic. Still, they do not want to spend extra money to build a bigger highway than they need.

CHAPTER THREE

Building a Road

Building a road happens in four steps. For a long road, builders work on one piece of the road at a time. They finish all the steps before they move on to the next piece.

Step One: Bridges and Tunnels

Roads and highways sometimes need special structures. If a road is going to cross over another road, or a river, it needs a bridge. If it is going to go through a rocky hill, it needs a tunnel.

A machine called an excavator (digger) clears away small hills from the path of the new road.

Builders usually start making these structures right away. If no new structures are needed, builders go straight to the next step.

Step Two: Clearing and Grading

The land where the road will go has to be cleared. This means getting rid of buildings, old roads, or trees. Clearing the path for a road can be a big job. Builders might use dynamite to blow up buildings.

A grader makes the newly cleared roadway smooth and flat.

They might cut down many trees and haul them away. If the road goes through open country, clearing is easier.

After the path is clear, the road builders grade it. They use bulldozers and other earthmoving machines to make it level and straight.

Road builders cannot get rid of every hill. Small hills, though, are bulldozed away. The dirt from those hills may be mixed with gravel to fill in low places. The builders make a roadway slope down a little bit from the center to both edges. This lets rainwater run off the road.

Next, the roadway is scraped to smooth out bumps and fill in holes. This is done with a machine called a **grader**. It has a long blade across the front, with a flat edge. A driver moves the grader slowly along the right of way.

Step Three: Paving

Once the roadway is graded, it can be paved. The roadway is given pavement, a smooth surface that protects it from rain.

Heavy rollers are used to flatten down fresh asphalt and chipseal.

The pavement lets cars and trucks travel faster than on dirt or gravel.

One of the last steps in building a road is painting on the lines that will guide traffic.

Some streets and highways are paved with concrete. This is the longest-lasting pavement. Builders can cut small lines or grooves into concrete. These let tires grip the surface of the road for safe driving.

The other main pavement today is asphalt concrete, a mixture of asphalt and concrete. This is called **blacktop** because it is dark in color. It costs less than concrete but does not last as long.

Roads with low traffic may be paved with **chipseal**. Builders spread asphalt on the roadway. On top of that they spread a coating of small pebbles. Then a machine with a heavy metal roller moves along the road, pressing the pebbles into the asphalt.

Step Four: Finishing

The last step in building a road is putting in the details. Road builders use special trucks to paint the yellow and white traffic lines onto the road. They put up light posts. They make sure that all parts of the design, such as safety railings, are in place.

Once the road is finished, there may be a special event to open it. A mayor or governor might cut a ribbon and make a speech. Now the new road is ready to be used.

CHAPTER **FOUR**

Roads in Use

The United States has more than four million miles of roads. That's enough road to drive to the Moon and back almost seventeen times!

More than two and half million miles of road in the United States are paved. This includes almost a quarter of a million miles in the National Highway System.

The rest of America's roads do not have pavement. Some are made of packed dirt. Others have a coat of

Many of the world's dirt roads are on farms. On this Japanese farm, rice grows on both sides of the road.

gravel over the packed dirt. Most dirt roads do not cover long distances. They are inside parks or in farmland.

Famous Roads

Some roads are famous. They may be fun to drive on, or have beautiful scenery, or be dangerous— or all three.

The most famous road in the city of San Francisco is Lombard Street. It snakes down a steep hill in a series of zigzags. It has been called "the crookedest street in the world."

This twisty mountain road in China has been called "the most dangerous road in the world."

A road in China has been called "the most dangerous in the world." It is the Guoliang Tunnel Road. It hugs the side of a steep mountain cliff and is only twelve feet wide. A handful of villagers built the road in the 1970s to connect their village to the outside world. Now this difficult road is a tourist attraction!

Route 66 was a famous American highway. Built in the 1920s, it ran from Chicago to California. Many Americans took this road to the western states. A popular song called "Route 66" named many cities that the highway passed through. Parts of Route 66 still remain in a few states.

The world's highest paved road between two countries is in Asia. This engineering wonder is called the Karakoram Highway. It runs through a mountain range to connect China and Pakistan. At its highest point the highway is 15,397 feet above sea level.

Roads of the Future?

Some road builders have exciting plans for the future. One idea is to paint lines on roads with paint that glows in the dark. This would help drivers stay on the road at night.

Another idea is to make roads out of solar panels strong enough to be driven on. The solar panels could make heat to melt ice and snow from the roads. They could also make electricity to run traffic lights and even homes and businesses.

With more and more people driving electric cars, some road builders are designing pavement with magnets in it. This would let people charge their cars with power while they drive.

Roads have been around for a long time. They will be part of our world for a long time to come.

The sun sets over the Mojave Desert in California. Route 66 once carried thousands of people to the American West.

GLOSSARY

asphalt A dark, sticky form of oil (like tar); when used to pave roads, asphalt is usually mixed with concrete to form asphalt-concrete.

blacktop Asphalt-concrete pavement, which is dark in color.

chipseal Pavement made by pressing small pebbles or bits of broken pavement into wet asphalt.

civil engineer An engineer who makes bridges, dams, roads, and other structures for the public to use.

concrete A blend of sand, gravel, cement, and water that is hard and strong when it dries.

engineer Someone who uses science to plan and build things.

geologist A scientist who studies geology, the subject of the earth and what it is made of.

grade To smooth out the bumps in a road and make it as flat and level as possible.

grader Machine with a long, straight-edged blade in front that is driven along a roadway to make it smooth.

gravel Small pieces of stone, all of them about the same size.

pave To cover something with a flat surface, called paving or a pavement.

road A line or route of travel, on land, that has been worked on to make it more than a simple path; traffic can move more easily on a road than on the land around it.

surveyor Someone trained to use tools to measure land and match it exactly to maps; surveyors mark out the line of a new road and make sure that the road-builders stay on track.

traffic Anything that travels on roads, including people, cars, and trucks.

FIND OUT MORE

Books

Macken, JoAnn E. *Building a Road*.
Minneapolis, MN: Capstone, 2008.

Sutton, Sally. *Roadwork*.
Somerville, MA: Candlewick, 2011.

Vestergaard, Hope. *Digger, Dozer, Dumper*.
Somerville, MA: Candlewick, 2013.

Websites

How a Road Gets Built

www.virginiadot.org/projects/pr-howroadblt.asp

How to Build an Interstate

www.fhwa.dot.gov/interstate/brainiacs
/buildinterstate.htm

How to Build a Road: A 19th Century Primer

xroads.virginia.edu/~Hyper/DETOC/transport/how.html

INDEX

Page numbers in **boldface** are illustrations. Entries in **boldface** are glossary terms.

ABOUT THE AUTHOR

Rebecca Stefoff has written books for young readers on many topics in science, technology, and history. She is the author of the six-volume series Is It Science? (Cavendish Square, 2014) and the four-volume series Animal Behavior Revealed (Cavendish Square, 2014). She also wrote *The Telephone*, *The Camera*, *Submarines*, *The Microscope and Telescope*, and *Robots* for Cavendish Square's Great Inventions series. Stefoff lives in Portland, Oregon. You can learn more about Stefoff and her books for young people at www.rebeccastefoff.com.